Reconciliation With God

Timeless Truth: Reconciliation With God

Published by Love Worth Finding Ministries, Inc.
2941 Kate Bond Rd
Memphis TN 38133-4017
(800) 274-5683

Concept and copy by Deborah Wade with contributions from Mike Jarvis.

Printed in the United States of America

QUESTIONS

EVERYTHING TO GAIN, NOTHING TO LOSE

You've got questions and you should ask them. God's not afraid of your questions. If you're truly seeking to know whether He's real and, if so, how you can know Him, He will reveal Himself to you. Don't stop asking questions until your heart is satisfied with the Truth.

This little book won't answer all your questions. It may lead to more questions. But it's a good place to start because the answers are derived straight from the Bible.

The Bible is God's Word to Man. The Bible is not presumptive of its readers: anyone can pick it up and read it. You may come to it from a position of disbelief, defiance, distrust or devotion, and it will tell you the same thing—that God created you, knows everything about you (the good and the ugly), and paid the ultimate price so you can be reconciled to Him and enjoy an intimate relationship with Him for all eternity.

Read thoughtfully. Reflect and journal. And enjoy the QR codes that are included in these pages to lead you to other helpful resources.

Now, ask those questions!

About God

DOES GOD EXIST?

"In the beginning God created the heavens and the earth. The earth was without form, and void; and darkness was on the face of the deep" (Genesis 1:1-2a).

Science can neither prove nor disprove God. Each individual asks and answers for himself, "Did the Universe come from nothing or from intelligent design?" If you answer "nothing," the next question is, "How do you know?" Your intelligence would have to be greater than the Universe to make that claim.

But if you answer, "Someone intelligent who is greater than the Universe, Someone with originating power Man does not possess, must have set everything in motion," that leads to the question "Who? ...Who has the power to create everything out of nothing when Man can only change the form of something already in existence?"

The Bible answers that question matter-of-factly.

From the very first words of the Bible, God is not argued, explained, or defended. He is simply presented. There is neither an explanation for the existence of God nor an attempt to prove His existence. He simply *is*.

The Bible says He created Man. We are His because of that creation and we have an obligation to Him. Not only that, but God has an obligation to us. The Bible states that He is a faithful Creator. (See 1 Peter 4:19.) When God brought us into this Universe, He did not make us to abandon us.

"We talk about how He's got the whole world in His hands. Friend, He's got the whole wide Universe in His hands. He's the one who spoke it into existence." ADRIAN ROGERS

 RESOURCE: Listen to Pastor Adrian Rogers' message based on Genesis 1:1, *How to Have a True Foundation.*

WHO IS GOD?

"And the Spirit of God was hovering over the face of the waters" (Genesis 1:2b).

"Then God said, 'Let Us make man in Our image, according to Our likeness'" (Genesis 1:26a).

"In the beginning was the Word, and the Word was with God, and the Word was God. He was in the beginning with God. All things were made through Him, and without Him nothing was made that was made" (John 1:1-3)."

God has a triune nature. He is one God in three persons. You can recognize those persons in the Scriptures above. The Spirit of God in Genesis 1:2b is God the Holy Spirit. The God speaking in Genesis 1:26 is God the Father. The Word who was with God in the beginning in John 1:1-3 is God the Son.

The Father, Son, and Holy Spirit are three distinct persons, all fully God. Yet together, they are one God.

The Trinity taught in the Bible is beyond our comprehension. We can't fully understand how God can be three in one. But the fact that it is beyond our understanding doesn't make it untrue.

While we can't understand the Trinity, God's nature is reflected in the order He established for this world.

Space consists of height, width, and depth. You can't have one without the other. Time is divided into past, present, and future. You cannot have one without the other. Time is triune. Space is triune. Man is triune. We're made in the image of

God—body, soul, and spirit. The soul consists of the mind, will, and emotions; the spirit is unique to Man and is the part of our nature through which we can know God.

"With my spirit I have spiritual life and I know the world above me; with my soul I have psychological life and I know the world around me; with my body I have physical life and I'm related to the world beneath me." ADRIAN ROGERS

 RESOURCE: Listen to the message, *The Value of a Soul.*

WHAT DOES GOD WANT FROM ME?

"For You formed my inward parts; You covered me in my mother's womb" (Psalm 139:13).

"I will praise You, for I am fearfully and wonderfully made." (Psalm 139:14a).

"How precious also are Your thoughts to me, O God! How great is the sum of them! If I should count them, they would be more in number than the sand; when I awake, I am still with You" (Psalm 139:17-18).

God created you to be someone He can love and who will love Him. God made you in His image: to know Him, to love Him, and to have fellowship with Him.

God wants a relationship with you.

If you're an evolutionist and an atheist, then you'll see yourself as an orphan of the apes. But if you see yourself as Almighty God's creation—with a purpose—it changes everything.

Read Psalm 139 and you will find not only that God created you but also that you exist for a purpose.

You will discover that He made you and knew you before you were born and that you are constantly in His heart. His thoughts toward you are greater than all the grains of sand in all the oceans and beaches and deserts of Earth.

The King James Version of the Bible says of your creation, "For Thou hast possessed my reins." The reins of a horse guide it. God wants to be with you and guide you throughout your life so that you can enjoy the specific purposes for which He made you.

You're not an accident. You didn't evolve from pond scum. God formed you in your mother's womb. You are special. You are unique.

Your first purpose is always to know God and to enjoy Him today, tomorrow, and forever. Your purposes are discovered through your knowledge and enjoyment of God, through prayer, through your study of God's Word, and through the service to which He directs you.

"God has a purpose and plan for me that
no one else can fulfill." ADRIAN ROGERS

 RESOURCE: Listen to the audio message,
Why Do I Exist?

IF GOD IS GOOD, WHY IS THERE SO MUCH SUFFERING?

"For our light affliction, which is but for a moment, is working for us a far more exceeding and eternal weight of glory, while we do not look at the things which are seen, but at the things which are not seen. For the things which are seen are temporary, but the things which are not seen are eternal" (2 Corinthians 4:17-18).

This is a question many have wrestled with. For those dealing with suffering, it's also a very personal question. And while the Bible doesn't give us all the answers, it does give us insight.

The Bible makes it clear that evil and suffering were not present when God created the world. In Genesis 1:31, we read, "Then God saw everything that He had made, and indeed it was very good. So the evening and the morning were the sixth day."

God gave Man free will. When Man (Adam and Eve) chose to eat the fruit God had forbidden, sin and suffering entered the world. Death, disease, trouble, and tribulation would now be a part of life.

Thankfully, that's not the end of the story. God put into place a plan by which He Himself, in the person of Jesus Christ, would overcome sin and death and make a way for people to spend eternity in relationship with Him. That plan will come to full fruition when Jesus Christ comes again for His bride, the Church.

Until then, God is sovereign over all suffering and evil, and nothing happens without God expressly allowing it to happen. And even though we can't know all that God is doing through suffering and evil, we can be sure of one thing: God uses the pain we experience for both our good and His glory.

As it says in Romans 8:28, "And we know that all things work together for good to those who love God, to those who are called according to His purpose."

A day is coming when all suffering and evil will end. When Jesus comes back, He is going to destroy sin, Satan, and suffering. Death will be eradicated, and the Lord will create a new Heaven and a new Earth. There will be no more sorrow or sadness. That is our ultimate hope.

> "The joy of the Lord isn't there to remove the pain; the joy of the Lord is there to help me bear it." ADRIAN ROGERS

RECOMMENDED: Consider using the Bible study, "How to Weather the Storms of Life," for yourself or for your small group.

IF GOD CREATED EVERYONE, ARE ALL PEOPLE GOD'S CHILDREN?

"Those who are the children of the flesh, these are not the children of God; but the children of the promise are counted as the seed" (Romans 9:8).

All people are God's creation. And Jesus took great care to let us know that God loves the entire world. (See John 3:16.)

In Romans 9:8, the Apostle Paul tells us that only those who know and love God through His Son, Jesus Christ, are children of "the promise," that is, the spiritual Children of Abraham, to whom God promised spiritual riches.

The Bible tells us we must be "born again" to become children of God. Why? All people are born as sinners, a condition which separates us from God and defines us as spiritually dead and as "...by nature objects of wrath..." (Ephesians 2:1-3).

Those who come into relationship with Jesus Christ—admitting and turning from sin and receiving God's forgiveness—are born again. Now spiritually alive, they are children of God who desire to do the will of their Father.

Jesus said of those who do not know God, "If God were your Father, you would love Me, for I proceeded forth and came from God; nor have I come of Myself, but He sent Me" (John 8:42). He told the Pharisees, "You are of your father the devil, and the desires of your father you want to do" (John 8:44a).

The Bible says in 1 John 3:10: "In this the children of God and the children of the devil are manifest: Whoever does not practice righteousness is not of God, nor is he who does not love his brother."

RESOURCE: Listen to Adrian Rogers' message, *Birthmarks of the Believer.*

WHAT DOES IT MEAN TO BE ADOPTED INTO GOD'S FAMILY?

"For as many as are led by the Spirit of God, these are sons of God. For you did not receive the spirit of bondage again to fear, but you received the Spirit of adoption by whom we cry out, "Abba, Father." The Spirit Himself bears witness with our spirit that we are children of God, and if children, then heirs—heirs of God and joint heirs with Christ, if indeed we suffer with Him, that we may also be glorified together" (Romans 8:14-17).

Those who come into relationship with Jesus are adopted into God's family and are given full rights as sons and daughters of God.

Ephesians 1:3-14 has adoption as its theme. The people of Ephesus to whom Ephesians was written would have understood clearly what it means to be a slave without a family or an orphan without hope and what it means to be adopted into a family headed by a generous father. They would have been overjoyed by this letter telling them that God's children are no longer orphans but are fully vested in God's family and have redemption through the blood of Jesus, forgiveness of sins because of the grace of Jesus, and wisdom and insight into the mystery of God's will. These children are united with God and with one another as brothers and sisters, are sealed with God's promised Holy Spirit, and have obtained the guarantee of an eternal inheritance.

As earthly children, we eventually inherit what our parents leave behind for us after their death. When we become children of God, we inherit nothing less than the Kingdom of God!

Even in this earthly life, children of God are already reaping the rewards of inheritance by having peace with God through the sacrifice of His Son on the cross. They are already enjoying the gift of God's indwelling Holy Spirit which empowers them to live for Him in the present. They have the right to go to God in prayer as "Abba," which means "Daddy," and they have a salvation that is secure for all eternity. (See Hebrews 7:24-25.)

> "God's children have read the last chapter. We know how it's going to end." ADRIAN ROGERS

RESOURCE: Want more? Read the article, "How Can You Be in God's Family?"

About Jesus

WHO IS JESUS?

"For by Him all things were created that are in heaven and that are on earth, visible and invisible, whether thrones or dominions or principalities or powers. All things were created through Him and for Him" (Colossians 1:16).

The Bible tells us that Jesus is the "only begotten Son of God," (John 3:18) and that He walked among us both fully human and fully divine. Jesus is the Creator of all things. He Himself could not be created because all things were created by Him.

According to Colossians 1:16, it was Jesus, the Second Person of the Trinity, at work during Creation. Whether things in Heaven or things on Earth, everything was made *by* Jesus and *for* Jesus.

Jesus is the very image of God. The word image here means the exact representation and likeness of God. Sometimes when we are photographed, we lament, "Oh, that's not a very good picture of me...." But God says Jesus is the very image of Himself. (See Colossians 1:15.) When we look at Jesus, we are seeing what God is like.

The Bible says that Jesus is the only person to have ever lived a perfect, sinless life. (See 2 Corinthians 5:21.) When He died on the cross, He took on all our sins so that we could be forgiven and have His sinless righteousness.

After making payment for our sins, Jesus was in the grave for three days. Then He rose from the dead, demonstrating that He had conquered both sin and death, which is the penalty for sin.

Now Jesus is reigning in Heaven. Someday He will return to Earth to judge the living and the dead, to destroy sin and Satan, and to make all things new.

"Jesus is Lord. We didn't vote Him in, and we won't vote Him out." ADRIAN ROGERS

RESOURCE: Watch Pastor Rogers' message, *Who is Jesus?*

IS THERE HISTORICAL EVIDENCE FOR JESUS' LIFE?

"I came forth from the Father and have come into the world. Again, I leave the world and go to the Father" (John 16:28).

Even if you don't believe that Jesus is the Son of God, there are many proofs that He walked the face of the Earth as a real person.

First, there is the existence of Christianity itself. To believe that Christianity sprung up around someone who never existed stretches the limits of imagination. There has never been a major religion for which the founder did not exist.

Second, even outside the Bible, there are numerous references to Jesus that indicate He was a real person. In the first century, a Roman historian named Tacitus wrote about Jesus' suffering under Pontius Pilate. The Jewish historian Josephus mentions Jesus in his writings from 93 A.D., which was approximately 60 years after the time Jesus was crucified by Pilate. Suetonius, who was the chief secretary to Emperor Hadrian wrote of a man named Chrestus (or Christ) who lived during the first century.

But perhaps most importantly, there were many eyewitnesses to the life, death, and resurrection of Jesus of Nazareth. In the four gospels, we encounter many different people who had their lives totally transformed by Jesus. He was publicly crucified in front of hundreds of people. And when He rose from the dead, He was seen multiple times by different groups of people, including a group as large as 500.

So yes, there is a large amount of evidence that Jesus is real. But beyond that, there is significant proof that He truly is the Son of God.

"Friend, the more I walk with Him, the more the Holy Spirit of God whispers to my heart, 'He's the one. He is the one. He is the one.' ...You say, 'Well, Adrian, you haven't proven anything to me.' I don't intend to prove anything to you. ...Jesus is more real to me than you are." ADRIAN ROGERS

RESOURCE: Read the article, "Who is Jesus? Do you have an answer?"

WHY IS JESUS' VIRGIN BIRTH SO IMPORTANT?

"Therefore the Lord Himself will give you a sign: Behold, the virgin shall conceive and bear a Son, and shall call His name Immanuel" (Isaiah 7:14).

"And the Word became flesh and dwelt among us, and we beheld His glory, the glory as of the only begotten of the Father, full of grace and truth" (John 1:14).

When our ancestor Adam sinned in the Garden of Eden, he dragged the entire human race down with him. Our relationship with God was lost through Adam. He sold it out to Satan. We're all blood-related descendants of Adam, and "In Adam, all die" (1 Corinthians 15:22a). Adam became a slave of Satan, and the son of a slave is a slave himself.

We're all sons of Adam. We receive his sinful nature by our natural birth. The burden of sin is upon us.

Here's where the Virgin Birth comes in. Jesus could not physically be a son of Adam. If He were, Adam's sinful blood would have been in His veins. He would have been a slave to Satan, just like every other son of Adam. He had to be the Son of God. Therefore, He was born of a virgin, sired by the Holy Spirit of God, to be sinless.

But Jesus also had to be a human being to pay the sin debt, "without the shedding of blood there is no remission" (Hebrews 9:22b). Therefore, He had to be the God-Man.

This is redemption: He came as He did, born of a virgin, to be what He was—sinless. He was what He was—sinless—to do what He did—die for our sins. A sinner could die for no one else's sin but his own. He died for our sins to be our substitute that we might be what we are—sons and daughters of God. He came to Earth that we might go to Heaven.

Thank God for the Virgin Birth! It's not incidental or mythological; it's the foundation stone of the Christian faith. God became man, buying back what the first Adam lost.

"He was born of a virgin that we might
be born again." ADRIAN ROGERS

RESOURCE: Watch the message,
Three Miracle Births.

IS JESUS THE ONLY WAY TO GOD?

"For it pleased the Father that in Him all the fullness should dwell" (Colossians 1:19).

"He [Jesus] is the image of the invisible God, the firstborn over all creation" (Colossians 1:15).

"All things have been delivered to Me by My Father, and no one knows the Son except the Father. Nor does anyone know the Father except the Son, and the one to whom the Son wills to reveal Him" (Matthew 11:27).

There is only one true God. And there is only one way to that one God: through Jesus Christ.

ONLY JESUS REVEALS THE FATHER. God is unseeable. Because He is infinite, He is unknowable. Because He is holy, He is unapproachable. There is no way we could come to or understand God by reason, religion, or ritual. We must know God by revelation. Somebody must take us by the hand and introduce us to God, and Jesus alone does this. You can know God as Creator, as sovereign—that is, you can know about Him. But you cannot know Him, and have intimate fellowship with Him, except through Jesus Christ, the Son of God.

ONLY JESUS RULES THE UNIVERSE. "For by Him all things were created that are in heaven and that are on earth, visible and invisible" (Colossians 1:16a). Jesus made every angel and every tree. The baby in Matthew 1 is the mighty God of Genesis 1. The baby in the manger was the God who spoke the Universe into existence.

ONLY JESUS RECONCILES THE LOST. "For it pleased the Father that in Him all the fullness should dwell, and by Him to reconcile all things to Himself, by Him, whether things on earth or things in heaven, having made peace through the blood of His cross" (Colossians 1:19-20). God, the mighty maker, died for man, the creature. It is Christ's deity that makes His death meaningful. He made the world with a word, but He saved it with His precious blood.

Eastern religions believe that life is circular—if you didn't do it right the first time, you get another chance. But the Bible teaches that history is linear, that we are headed toward a climax, a purpose. It was all made for Jesus.

> "If you wonder what this world is coming to, it is coming to Jesus!" **ADRIAN ROGERS**

RESOURCE: View Adrian Rogers' full message, *Jesus, the One and Only.*

DID JESUS CLAIM TO BE GOD?

"Again the high priest asked Him, saying to Him, 'Are You the Christ, the Son of the Blessed?' Jesus said, 'I am. And you will see the Son of Man sitting at the right hand of the Power, and coming with the clouds of heaven.'" Then the high priest tore his clothes and said, "'What further need do we have of witnesses? You have heard the blasphemy! What do you think?' And they all condemned Him to be deserving of death" (Mark 14:61-64).

Jesus' claim to be the Son of Man and the Son of the Blessed (God) was the reason the Jewish leaders sought to have Him crucified. When Jesus said, "I am," He was identifying Himself as God with the same name by which God identified Himself to Moses in the burning bush. (See Exodus 3:14.)

Jesus used the same name for Himself in a conversation with the Pharisees in the Book of John: "'Your father Abraham rejoiced to see My day, and he saw it and was glad.' Then the Jews said to Him, 'You are not yet fifty years old, and have You seen Abraham?' Jesus said to them, 'Most assuredly, I say to you, before Abraham was, I AM'" (John 8:56-58).

In that instance, many of those in the crowd picked up stones, intending to kill Him for blaspheming by claiming to be God, but Jesus eluded them because it was not yet His time to die.

In John 10, Jesus again told His listeners that He and the Father are one. Again, He was questioned, and again He was threatened with arrest for the sin of blasphemy.

In John 14, Philip asked of Jesus: "'Lord, show us the Father, and it is sufficient for us.' Jesus said to him, 'Have I been with you so long, and yet you have not known Me, Philip? He who has seen Me has seen the Father; so how can you say, "Show us the Father"? Do you not believe that I am in the Father, and the Father in Me? The words that I speak to you I do not speak on My own authority; but the Father who dwells in Me does the works. Believe Me that I am in the Father and the Father in Me, or else believe Me for the sake of the works themselves.'" (vs. 8-11).

In Mark 2, Jesus healed a paralytic man and forgave his sins. This was called blasphemy by the scribes who were present because they knew that only God has authority to forgive sin. (See Isaiah 43:25.) Luke also recorded this claim in Luke 5:20.

In Matthew 14:33 and 28:9, Jesus received the kind of worship Jews reserved for God alone.

And who could forget the worship Jesus received as Messiah in Luke 19 during His triumphal entry into Jerusalem on Palm Sunday? "Then, as He was now drawing near the descent of the Mount of Olives, the whole multitude of the disciples began to rejoice and praise God with a loud voice for all the mighty works they had seen, saying: '"Blessed is the King who comes in the name of the Lord!" Peace in heaven and glory in the highest!' And some of the Pharisees called to Him from the crowd, 'Teacher, rebuke Your disciples.' But He answered and said to them, 'I tell you that if these should keep silent, the stones would immediately cry out'" (Luke 19:37-40).

Jesus was saying then, and would say to us now, that He is God and will receive worship, whether from men and women or from the very elements He created.

"To worship is your greatest need. To worship is your ultimate privilege. To worship is your supreme duty." ADRIAN ROGERS

RESOURCE: Listen to Pastor Rogers' message, *How to Keep the Wonder in Your Worship.*

DID JESUS LIVE A SINLESS LIFE?

"And you know that He was manifested to take away our sins, and in Him there is no sin" (1 John 3:5).

"...you were not redeemed with corruptible things, like silver or gold, from your aimless conduct received by tradition from your fathers, but with the precious blood of Christ, as of a lamb without blemish and without spot" (1 Peter 1:18-19).

"Pilate then went out again, and said to them, 'Behold, I am bringing Him out to you, that you may know that I find no fault in Him'" (John 19:4).

Jesus lived a perfectly sinless life on this Earth and remains perfect. Jesus is simultaneously 100% God and 100% Man. He is the God Man.

Unlike us, Jesus was born without sin. Isaiah 7:14 says, "Therefore the Lord Himself will give you a sign: Behold, the virgin shall conceive and bear a son, and shall call his name Immanuel." Matthew 1:20b says, "...'Joseph, son of David, do not be afraid to take Mary as your wife, for that which is conceived in her is of the Holy Spirit.'" Jesus was not conceived by a sinful man but by the perfection of the Holy Spirit of God. This allowed Him to be born sinless.

Sin has been passed down through the man since Adam because Adam sinned. "Therefore, just as through one man [Adam] sin entered the world, and death through sin, and thus death spread to all men, because all sinned" (Romans 5:12). Since

Jesus was born and remained sinless, He could then offer the gift of righteousness to all through His righteousness. "For if by the one man's offense death reigned through the one, much more those who received abundance of grace and the gift of righteousness will reign in life through the One, Jesus Christ" (Romans 5:17).

From birth to the cross, Jesus lived a perfectly sinless life. He was tempted as we are, but He fought sin perfectly using prayer, the Word of God, and submission to God's will. He understands our dilemma with sin and its struggles because He too faced those struggles. Hebrews 4:15 says, "For we do not have a High Priest [Jesus] who cannot sympathize with our weaknesses, but was in all points tempted as we are, yet without sin." Only on the Cross was sin a part of Jesus, and that wasn't even His own sin, but ours! Second Corinthians 5:21 says, "For He [God the Father] made Him who knew no sin [Jesus] to be sin for us, that we might become the righteousness of God in Him."

Because Jesus loves us, He came born of a virgin, lived a sinlessly perfect life, and died the death we should have so that we could trade our sin for His righteousness and receive the gift of salvation.

"We don't do anything perfectly,
but sin." ADRIAN ROGERS

 RESOURCE: For more about the sinless life of Christ, read the article, "The Messianic Prophecies of Jesus."

WHY DID JESUS HAVE TO DIE?

"And according to the law almost all things are purified with blood, and without the shedding of blood there is no remission" (Hebrews 9:22).

Jesus died to pay the penalty for our sin.

The first picture we see regarding the shedding of blood is in Genesis 3:21 as God is dealing with Adam and Eve after they sinned. It says, "Also for Adam and his wife the Lord God made tunics of skin, and clothed them." Animals had to be killed, the shedding of blood had to take place, to make tunics of skin to hide their nakedness (to hide or cover their sin).

Later, Moses would write the law God gave him, and it would contain several types of sacrifices. One would be for the sin of the people on the Day of Atonement. An unspotted or unblemished lamb would be slain, and its blood would be sprinkled on the altar as a symbol of covering the people's sin. Old Testament sacrifices foreshadowed the true Lamb of God, Jesus, and His perfect sacrifice for our sin.

Throughout the Old Testament, spelled out in Scripture and gleaned from historical accounts, we find pictures of salvation. For example, God commanded Noah to build an ark for the saving of his family and of the creatures God created. The ark is a picture of Jesus Christ, through whom we are saved from the waters of sin and judgment. Abraham was called to sacrifice His only son, Isaac, but at the last minute, God intervened and provided a ram for the sacrifice. This account foreshadowed Jesus as our substitutionary sacrifice. When the

Israelites were wandering in the desert following their exodus from Egypt, they worshipped in a specific way in a tent called the Tabernacle that was designed by God to tell the story of Jesus' death on our behalf.

God has been reaching out to Man from the first Book of Genesis through the final Book of Revelation. Jesus' death, burial, and resurrection, prophesied in the Old Testament and realized in the New Testament, made it possible for all men to be reconciled to God through salvation. Only those who receive Jesus as Lord and Savior are granted this salvation. "For God did not appoint us to wrath, but to obtain salvation through our Lord Jesus Christ" (1 Thessalonians 5:9).

"What is the difference between manmade religion and true salvation? Man tries to build from earth to Heaven. True salvation reaches down from Heaven to man. That's the difference." ADRIAN ROGERS

RESOURCE: Read the article, "Jesus Died to Give You Eternal Life."

RECOMMENDED: Order the book, "Seeing Jesus in Unexpected Places," which is based on Pastor Rogers' messages describing the design of the Tabernacle.

WHY IS JESUS CALLED THE LAMB OF GOD?

"But you, Bethlehem Ephrathah, though you are little among the thousands of Judah, yet out of you shall come forth to Me the One to be Ruler in Israel, whose goings forth are from of old, from everlasting" (Micah 5:2).

"Joseph also went up from Galilee, out of the city of Nazareth, into Judea, to the city of David, which is called Bethlehem, because he was of the house and lineage of David, to be registered with Mary, his betrothed wife, who was with child. So it was, that while they were there, the days were completed for her to be delivered. And she brought forth her firstborn Son, and wrapped Him in swaddling cloths, and laid Him in a manger, because there was no room for them in the inn" (Luke 2:4-7).

We know that Micah is referencing a Person of the Trinity because His "goings forth are from old, from everlasting." It was understood by Old Testament scholars, including the chief priests and scribes of Jesus' day, that the Messiah would have His earthly beginnings in Bethlehem.

Bethlehem is a little village five and a half miles south of Jerusalem. We might never have heard of it had not Mary's little Lamb been born there. How fitting! For centuries the Jewish priests had been raising a special breed of lambs in Bethlehem, the best of which, the unblemished, were sacrificed during the Passover to atone for sin. In Luke, the perfect sacrifice, as prophesied, was born in a Bethlehem stable and laid in an animal trough. He would "atone" for all sin for all time. He would make it possible for us to be "at one" with God.

This atonement through the blood of the Lamb was foreshadowed in the Old Testament in the Book of Exodus when God instituted the first Passover meal: "Now the blood shall be a sign for you on the houses where you are. And when I see the blood, I will pass over you; and the plague shall not be on you to destroy you when I strike the land of Egypt" (Exodus 12:13).

The Passover, celebrated every year, gave the Israelites opportunity to look back at their time in Egypt (which is symbolic of sin) and forward to the coming of the Messiah, who would bring redemption through His righteousness. Jeremiah 23:5-6 says, "Behold, the days are coming," says the LORD, "That I will raise to David a Branch of righteousness; a King shall reign and prosper, and execute judgment and righteousness in the earth. In His days Judah will be saved, and Israel will dwell safely; now this is His name by which He will be called: THE LORD OUR RIGHTEOUSNESS."

The Passover lambs raised in Bethlehem were considered perfect, symbolic of righteousness before God. Even then, only the best of the best made the five-and-a-half-mile trip to Jerusalem for the Passover festival.

Jesus celebrated His last Passover meal with His Disciples, during which He instituted the taking of communion. As He offered the cup and the bread, "He said to them, 'This is My blood of the new covenant, which is shed for many" (Mark

14:24). "Likewise He also took the cup after supper, saying, 'This cup is the new covenant in My blood, which is shed for you'" (Luke 22:20).

This is the sequence of events for Jesus, the Lamb of God, and for the Passover lambs during the week before the crucifixion: Jesus enters Jerusalem through the Eastern Gate; the Passover lambs enter through the Sheep Gate. Jesus cleanses the temple; the Jewish people cleanse their homes of leaven (yeast), a symbol of sin. Jesus introduces the cup of "the new covenant in My blood, which is shed for you;" the Jewish people celebrate the Seder meal—retelling the story of the blood on the doorposts. Jesus is examined before Pilate; the Passover lambs are scrutinized. Jesus walks to Calvary; the priests sharpen their knives. Jesus commits His spirit to the Father; the Passover lambs have their chins lifted to the priests.

<blockquote>"Jesus came to reveal the character of God, not to display the grandeur of God." ADRIAN ROGERS</blockquote>

 RESOURCE: Pastor Rogers delivered three sets of messages under the title, *The Triumph of the Lamb*. You can listen to them here.

WHY IS JESUS CALLED THE GOOD SHEPHERD?

"'I am the good shepherd. The good shepherd gives His life for the sheep. But a hireling, he who is not the shepherd, one who does not own the sheep, sees the wolf coming and leaves the sheep and flees; and the wolf catches the sheep and scatters them. The hireling flees because he is a hireling and does not care about the sheep. I am the good shepherd; and I know My sheep, and am known by My own. As the Father knows Me, even so I know the Father; and I lay down My life for the sheep. And other sheep I have which are not of this fold; them also I must bring, and they will hear My voice; and there will be one flock and one shepherd. Therefore My Father loves Me, because I lay down My life that I may take it again. No one takes it from Me, but I lay it down of Myself. I have power to lay it down, and I have power to take it again. This command I have received from My Father" (John 10:11-18).

In the Book of John, Jesus called Himself "The Good Shepherd," intentionally referring to Himself in a way that His hearers, the Pharisees, would understand as a claim to be the Messiah foretold in Ezekiel 34. In that chapter, God rebukes the leaders of His flock for being poor shepherds and promises that the Sovereign Lord Himself will come to shepherd His flock.

He compares the Pharisees to a "hireling" or "hired hand" who doesn't really care about the sheep; this contrasts with Jesus, who will lay down His life for the sheep. In John 10:8, Jesus speaks of thieves and robbers who seek to enter the sheepfold stealthily. Again, this contrasts with Jesus the Messiah, who calls Himself the Door to the sheepfold.

Jesus said He would shepherd His flock, His followers, as well as others who would come under His care—those who would come to believe in Him in the Last Days, the time between His ascension into Heaven and His future Second Coming.

Carefully read Psalm 23 and you will get a picture of the Good Shepherd. Jesus' tenderness, righteousness, compassion, and courage can all be seen in this Psalm as He lovingly protects, provides for, and walks alongside His sheep.

At the end of Psalm 23, the Psalmist confidently states, "I will dwell in the house of the LORD forever," presenting a picture of eternal fellowship between himself and The Good Shepherd. In John 14:3, Jesus emphatically states to His followers, "I go and prepare a place for you, I will come again and receive you to Myself; that where I am, there you may be also." He also tells His followers just before His ascension into Heaven, "I am with you always, even to the end of the age" (Matthew 28:20b).

"Let the presence of Jesus guide you. Let the promises of Jesus gladden you. Let the power of Jesus guard you." ADRIAN ROGERS

 RECOMMENDED: Get *The LORD is My Shepherd* Gift Book by Adrian Rogers for yourself or for someone you love.

WHO CRUCIFIED JESUS?

"He is despised and rejected by men, a Man of sorrows and acquainted with grief. And we hid, as it were, our faces from Him; He was despised, and we did not esteem Him. Surely He has borne our griefs and carried our sorrows; yet we esteemed Him stricken, smitten by God, and afflicted. But He was wounded for our transgressions, He was bruised for our iniquities; the chastisement for our peace was upon Him, and by His stripes we are healed. All we like sheep have gone astray; we have turned, every one, to his own way; and the LORD has laid on Him the iniquity of us all" (Isaiah 53:3-6).

The prophecy above about Jesus' crucifixion was written about 700 years before the birth of Jesus, at a time when crucifixion had not yet been invented as a cruel instrument of death.

The Jewish leaders convinced the people to call for Jesus' crucifixion. Pilate washed his hands ceremonially but still handed the Lord over to be crucified. The Roman soldiers scourged, spat upon, and nailed Jesus to the cross. But it would be foolish to blame either the Jews or the Romans for Jesus' death.

Jesus laid down His life willingly, so in one sense no one can be held responsible for the death of Jesus on the cross. The crucifixion was God's plan and one that could not be stopped.

But in another sense, everyone who has ever lived—since we all are sinners—is responsible. When Jesus carried His cross up the Hill of Golgotha, the collective sin of every person across the centuries past—as well as the years to come until Christ returns—was laid on Jesus' shoulders.

Our sins were the nails that held Jesus to the cross. Our hard hearts were the hammers that drove those nails. We are all guilty.

Mel Gibson, who produced "The Passion of the Cross," acted in only one small part of the film. There is a close-up in the film of someone driving the spike into the hand of Jesus Christ. Mel Gibson arranged that his was the forearm and the hand that held the hammer. He was saying, "I am guilty of the crucifixion of Jesus Christ." And God help us, so are we all.

> "As we call the roll at the cross, listen and you'll hear your name called." ADRIAN ROGERS

 RESOURCE: Pastor Rogers said it was our self-righteous religion, hard-hearted hypocrisy, cowardly compromise, and thoughtless conformity that drove us to crucify Jesus. Watch his message, *Who Crucified Jesus?*

WHAT IS THE EVIDENCE FOR JESUS' RESURRECTION?

"O Death, where is your sting? O Hades, where is your victory?" (1 Corinthians 15:55).

Over the centuries, many people have questioned whether the resurrection of Jesus actually occurred. It's an important question because all of Christianity hinges upon the resurrection. Unlike other religions, Christians don't place their hope in a set of teachings or beliefs. We place our hope in Jesus Himself. No resurrection means no Jesus. No Jesus means no Christianity.

So how can we be sure that the resurrection of Jesus really happened? How can we be confident that our faith is true and not based on an elaborate lie? Here are three proofs to consider:

THE TESTIMONY OF THE DISCIPLES. The disciples didn't expect Jesus to rise from the dead; they didn't even expect Him to die. They had witnessed Him die a slow, agonizing death and watched a Roman soldier thrust his spear into Jesus' side and pierce His heart. He was dead. End of story. After He died, they behaved as if He were never coming back. When the women who went to His tomb to anoint His body told the disciples they had seen the risen Christ, the disciples didn't believe them. But then Jesus appeared to all His disciples, proving to them He was indeed alive. They believed in the resurrection because they saw Jesus with their own eyes. They were transformed from scaredy cats hiding away from the world into bold evangelists willing to suffer and die for their conviction. James was beheaded. Stephen was stoned to death.

John was sent into exile. Peter was crucified upside down. Even doubting Thomas went to his death holding fast to the belief that Jesus was alive. Would the disciples have endured such suffering if Jesus hadn't risen from the dead? Absolutely not. People aren't willing to die for something they know isn't true.

THE SECURE TOMB. The Pharisees and religious leaders knew Jesus claimed He would rise from the dead. So, measures were taken to prevent that from happening. A heavy stone was rolled in front of the entrance to the tomb in which Jesus was buried. This stone most likely weighed several hundred pounds and required several people to move. The Pharisees placed a seal around the stone, probably made of clay. The seal would have been impressed with the Roman imperial seal. Anyone breaking the seal would incur the wrath of the Roman emperor. Guards were also placed around the tomb to prevent anyone from getting close to it. To get to the body of Jesus, someone would have to get past all the guards on duty and roll away a giant stone, all without making any noise. The disciples certainly weren't in any position to do this. They were in hiding. Furthermore, why would the disciples steal Jesus' body and then claim He had risen from the dead? It was those very claims after Jesus did rise from the dead that resulted in their being tortured and killed.

CHANGED LIVES. In addition to the historical proof that Jesus rose from the dead, there is also the fact that millions of people's lives have been dramatically changed by Jesus. Around the globe, the hopeless have received hope, the broken have received healing, and the lost have been found. The followers of Jesus didn't have political or military power. They didn't have access to the halls of influence. And yet the message of the risen Jesus spread around the globe, penetrating people groups, crossing language barriers, even transforming entire cultures—all despite significant opposition. The followers of Jesus faced consistent persecution. The leaders of powerful nations like Rome sought to exterminate Christians. Nero burned Christians alive, even using them as human torches. And yet the Gospel continued to spread. Rome is gone. The risen Jesus continues to change lives. The real question is, have you let Him change yours?

> "You will fall or rise on Jesus. Jesus will be to you a stepping-stone, or He will be a stumbling block." ADRIAN ROGERS

RESOURCE: Listen to the message, *The Resurrection Body.*

About a Relationship with God

WHAT'S THE DIFFERENCE BETWEEN BEING RELIGIOUS AND HAVING A RELATIONSHIP?

"Then I will give them a heart to know Me, that I am the LORD; and they shall be My people, and I will be their God, for they shall return to Me with their whole heart" (Jeremiah 24:7).

There is an enormous difference between religion and relationship. Religion says work, work, work, and maybe you will be rewarded. Religion speaks from afar to a so-called god who may or may not be paying attention to you. Religion is impersonal, leaving you where you are, empty and alone.

Relationship is so much more valuable. Consider three reasons:

RELATIONSHIP WITH GOD IS PERSONAL. Scripture reveals God as a triune being—God the Father, God the Son, and God the Holy Spirit. Scripture tells us the fullness of the Trinity dwells in each believer. It doesn't get any more personal than that. The Father dwells: "As God has said, 'I will dwell in them and walk among them. I will be their God and they shall be My people'" (2 Corinthians 6:16b). The Son dwells: "that Christ may dwell in your hearts through faith" (Ephesians 3:17a). The Holy Spirit dwells: "But if the Spirit of Him who raised Jesus from the dead dwells in you, He who raised Christ from the dead will also give life to your mortal bodies through His Spirit who dwells in you" (Romans 8:11).

RELATIONSHIP WITH GOD IS POSITIONAL. Believers are adopted by God: "But now, thus says the LORD, who created you, O Jacob, and He who formed you, O Israel: 'Fear not, for I have redeemed you; I have called you by your name; you are Mine'" (Isaiah 43:1). Believers have fellowship with family members of the household of faith: "So we, being many, are one body in Christ, and individually members of one another" (Romans 12:5).

RELATIONSHIP WITH GOD PROVIDES PROMISES! Those who know God are never alone: "...I will never leave you nor forsake you." (Hebrews 13:5b). God's children are guaranteed transformation: "...being confident of this very thing, that He who has begun a good work in you will complete it until the day of Jesus Christ" (Philippians 1:6). God's children have eternal life: "These things have I written to you who believe in the name of the Son of God, that you may know that you have eternal life, and that you may continue to believe in the name of the Son of God" (1 John 5:13).

God will be with His children forever and He will finish what He started in them. Oh, the vast difference between religion and relationship!

> "Christianity is not a religion; it is a vital relationship with Jesus Christ." ADRIAN ROGERS

RESOURCE: Watch Adrian Rogers' message, *How You Can Know God Personally.*

WHAT IS THE BIBLICAL DEFINITION OF SALVATION?

"For the wages of sin is death, but the gift of God is eternal life in Christ Jesus our Lord" (Romans 6:23).

Salvation means being saved by God from the wrath of God.

God is perfectly righteous. He created us to be in relationship with Him. But because God is holy He has no fellowship with sin.

When Adam and Eve sinned, they were separated from God. Death was introduced. Since Adam and Eve, all people have been born, and continue to be born, with sin natures, separated from God, deserving His wrath. So, God put into place a plan to save humanity from His wrath. From Genesis to Revelation, this plan, the Gospel, has been clearly communicated in God's Word, the Bible.

One of the best biblical descriptions of the Gospel is found in 1 Corinthians 15:3b-4: "...that Christ died for our sins according to the Scriptures, and that He was buried, and that He rose again the third day according to the Scriptures." First Corinthians 15:2a says this is the Gospel, "by which you are saved."

You experience salvation when the Holy Spirit convicts you that you are a sinner in need of a Savior, you believe that Jesus is that Savior, you confess that belief, and you "repent" or "turn from" sin.

The Bible says, "...if you confess with your mouth the Lord Jesus and believe in your heart that God has raised Him from the dead, you will be saved. For with the heart one believes unto righteousness, and with the mouth confession is made unto salvation" (Romans 10:9-10).

When this happens, you then receive peace with God the Father, instead of His wrath, all because of what God the Son did by dying in your place. You receive life eternal in relationship with the God who created you.

> "We don't have to go on a pilgrimage to
> find salvation, because Jesus Christ stepped
> out of Heaven to find us." ADRIAN ROGERS

RESOURCE: Watch the message, *Salvation.*

WHAT IF I DON'T REGRET MY SIN?

"But be doers of the word, and not hearers only, deceiving yourselves. For if anyone is a hearer of the word and not a doer, he is like a man observing his natural face in a mirror; for he observes himself, goes away, and immediately forgets what kind of man he was. But he who looks into the perfect law of liberty and continues in it, and is not a forgetful hearer but a doer of the work, this one will be blessed in what he does" (James 1:22-25).

If you understand what sin is, then you should know that you need forgiveness. Sin is a moral affront to a holy God. It's falling short. It's missing the mark of what He wanted for us, His creation.

All human beings are sinners by birth, by nature, by choice, and by practice. We have offended God, and because He is just, He must punish sin. And we deserve punishment! Yet, God loves us.

If you are truly seeking to know Jesus, then you need to take a look in the mirror. You cannot confess to God what you will not admit to yourself. Before you can accept Jesus as your Lord and Savior, you must look at your sin and see it's ugliness in the eyes of a perfect and holy God. Confess your sin and forsake it. Turn from the mirror where you saw your sin around to a life in which you forsake that sin. There is no repentance without brokenness. Jesus suffered and died on your behalf so that you could live for eternity in Heaven with the one true God who loves you and wants to forgive you.

The fact that a holy, perfect God would choose to love you and forgive you and send His Son to die for you should have you praising Him continually.

You need not live in constant regret. Once you have confessed and turned from your sin and accepted Jesus as both Savior and Lord, you will not want to continue sinning; you will want to live a life of obedience before God because you love Him. This does not mean you will live perfectly, but that you will have an ever-increasing desire to live in a way that pleases your Lord.

> "No one has ever sinned themselves beyond the love of God. Sin is not just breaking God's laws; it is breaking His heart." ADRIAN ROGERS

RESOURCE: Read the article, "Can God ever forgive me?"

WHAT IS A BORN-AGAIN CHRISTIAN?

"Jesus answered and said to him, 'Most assuredly, I say to you, unless one is born again, he cannot see the kingdom of God.' Nicodemus said to him, 'How can a man be born when he is old? Can he enter a second time into his mother's womb and be born?' Jesus answered, 'Most assuredly, I say to you, unless one is born of water and the Spirit, he cannot enter the kingdom of God'" (John 3:3-5).

The term "born again" is just as unique to us as it was to Nicodemus when Jesus spoke to him. Until you are born again, it is a foreign concept. However, it is a wonderful thing to discover! In the Scripture above, Jesus begins to explain to Nicodemus that being born again has nothing to do with physical birth and everything to do with spiritual birth. So, anyone of any age can be born again at any moment.

Jesus speaks of being born of both water and the Spirit. In John 3:6, Jesus says, "That which is born of the flesh is flesh, and that which is born of the Spirit is spirit." Jesus makes a distinction between the two to remind us that flesh (physical birth-born of water) is not eternal (See Genesis 3:19.), but our spirits are eternal, thus we need a Savior.

Jesus also speaks to the work of the Holy Spirit in the life of the believer. John 3:7-8 declares, "Do not marvel that I said to you, 'You must be born again.' The wind blows where it wishes, and you hear the sound of it, but cannot tell where it comes from and where it goes. So is everyone who was born of the Spirit."

We may not be able to tell where the Holy Spirit came from or where He is going, but we can see the effects of His actions in changed lives. We can hear these effects in the voices of those now proclaiming the Gospel instead of cursing it. We can feel the effects of the Holy Spirit's ministry as we faithfully pursue Christlikeness or as we experience love and care from fellow believers when we're going through difficult times. The wonder and awe of being born again, of being a Christian, is something that is freely available to all those who put their faith in Jesus alone for salvation. "For God so loved the world that he gave his only begotten Son, that whoever believes in Him should not perish but have everlasting life" (John 3:16).

> "When we are born again, we are born to win." ADRIAN ROGERS

RESOURCE: View Pastor Rogers' message, *Birthmarks of the Believer.*

WHAT IS FAITH?

"Now faith is the substance of things hoped for, the evidence of things not seen" (Hebrews 11:1).

Faith is not positive thinking. It is not following a hunch. It is not a feeling of optimism. It is not hoping for the best. All of these may be well and good, but they are not biblical faith.

"Faith is the substance of things hoped for." Substance means "solid ground." The English word substance gives the meaning of the Greek word hupostasis. It means there is something beneath us to stand upon. When we are living by faith, we are standing upon the solid rock.

Sometimes the materialist will say, "Don't talk to me about faith. Talk about real things." He means, of course, the things that can be experienced with the five senses—the things we can see, smell, hear, taste, or touch.

But are these the only things that are real? Paul reminded us that "the things which are seen are temporary; but the things which are not seen are eternal" (2 Corinthians 4:18b). Which is more real—that which is temporary or that which is eternal? Which is more substantial? Which is able to support you?

Faith is substance, and it is also evidence. "Faith is...the evidence of things not seen." This means that faith is the convincing proof that God will keep His Word. Evidence is the proof of unseen reality. There can be no evidence without the reality that gave rise to the evidence. If we understand this, we shall see the difference between real faith, based on the truth of God's Word, and synthetic faith, based on wishful thinking.

The prophets of synthetic faith say, "If you have enough faith, God will do anything for you. All you have to do is name it and claim it." That sounds good, but it bears little resemblance to biblical faith. We cannot legitimately claim it until God has named it.

Faith is our response to a revelation of God's will by His Word and His Spirit. "So then faith comes by hearing, and hearing by the word of God" (Romans 10:17). Faith is the evidence in our hearts that God has spoken and that He will act according to His Word.

"Faith is the response of the heart to the character of God." ADRIAN ROGERS

RESOURCE: Read the article, *Do You Live by Faith?*

WHY DOES GOD REQUIRE FAITH?

"But without faith it is impossible to please Him, for he who comes to God must believe that He is, and that He is a rewarder of those who diligently seek Him" (Hebrews 11:6).

We should have no greater aim in life than to please God. But there is no pleasing God without believing Him. Why is this so? Why is God so pleased with faith? Why didn't He just create us so that we would automatically believe in Him? Why doesn't He do something to prove Himself to us?

If God wanted to prove Himself, He could roll back the heavens and make Himself known with a display of His grandeur, might, and glory. But such displays would render faith unnecessary. One day, God will reveal Himself in just that way, not to save men, but to judge them: "...that at the name of Jesus every knee should bow, of those in heaven, and of those on earth, and of those under the earth, and that every tongue should confess that Jesus Christ is Lord, to the glory of God the Father" (Philippians 2:10-11).

God does not reveal Himself in that manner today because He wants us to respond to Him by faith. Why? Faith is a moral response to God's character. Faith gives God the honor due His name. God wants us to love Him not for what He can do, but for who He is. God refuses to bribe or overwhelm us to make us follow Him.

This helps us understand why Jesus came as He did. He came to reveal the character of God, not to display the grandeur of God. He left the glory that was inherently His in Heaven when He came to this Earth. Jesus did not ride out of Heaven in a jeweled chariot wearing regal robes and a diadem. He was born in a stable and reared in an obscure village as a carpenter's son. He lived a life of poverty and humility. It is true that He performed miracles, but not to gain followers. His miracles were works of mercy and revelation of truth, not cheap tricks or public relations stunts.

Jesus knew the mindset of the miracle-mongers, those who wanted a sign from Heaven so they could believe. Such people followed Him for a while. But when He preached to them about real commitment, they left Him. There were others who loved and followed Jesus sincerely. They did not follow Him for what He did, but rather for who He was. They responded by faith to His character and person.

The reason God honors faith is that faith honors God. Faith is a moral response to the character of God. It is faith that gives God pleasure.

"A true heart responds to God by faith like a healthy eye responds to light and a healthy ear responds to sound." ADRIAN ROGERS

RECOMMENDED: Get the booklet, "Does Jesus Still Do Miracles?"

DOES JESUS SAY I AM SAVED BY FAITH ALONE?

"For by grace you have been saved through faith, and that not of yourselves; it is the gift of God, not of works, lest anyone should boast" (Ephesians 2:8-9).

Grace Alone. Faith Alone. Grace alone means that God loves, forgives, and saves us not because of who we are or what we do, but because of the work of Christ.

Jesus Himself said you are saved by faith alone. Here are two scriptural examples of Jesus making this proclamation:

"Then He said to her, 'Your sins are forgiven'. And those who sat at the table with Him began to say to themselves 'Who is this who even forgives sins?' Then He said to the woman, 'Your faith has saved you. Go in peace'" (Luke 7:48-50).

"For God so loved the world that he gave his only begotten Son, that whoever believes in Him should not perish but have everlasting life" (John 3:16).

The word "faith" in the first verse is the Greek word *pistis*, and the word "believes" in the second verse is the Greek word *pisteuo*. Take notice that they have the same root-*pist*. John uses believes just as Paul uses the word faith in his epistles. The way John uses it gives it the same meaning as the word faith seen elsewhere in Scripture. Therefore, Jesus, using both words, is saying that we are saved by faith, in Him, alone.

All those who are saved desire to please Jesus and to obey His commands. They serve or work for God's glory. Their works do not bring salvation, but their works are evidence of God's Holy Spirit who indwells all true Christians.

> "Man is saved by faith alone, but the faith that saves is never alone." ADRIAN ROGERS

 RESOURCE: Listen to this message about faith and works, *The Autopsy of a Dead Faith*.

MUST I BE BAPTIZED TO BE SAVED?

"Therefore we are buried with Him through baptism into death, that just as Christ was raised from the dead by the glory of the Father, even so, we also should walk in newness of life" (Romans 6:4).

Baptism is not required for salvation. Baptism is a public declaration of faith in Jesus Christ and an act of obedience to His command.

DECLARATION OF FAITH As a public declaration of faith in Jesus Christ, baptism shows others that we have died to our old lives and have been raised to live new lives in Christ. Just as Jesus died and was buried, we lie back as a picture of death and go under the water as a picture of burial. Then, just as Jesus was raised to life on the third day, we come up out of the water as a picture of His resurrection. We do this in front of the church as a declaration of our faith.

ACT OF OBEDIENCE Baptism shows that we are ready to obey the call of Christ to a new way of life. Jesus was baptized Himself. You can read about it in all four of the Gospels: Matthew 3, Mark 1, Luke 3, and John 1. Jesus began His public ministry after He obediently went to John and was baptized. The same goes for us. We receive salvation, are baptized, and then begin ministry as children of God.

BAPTISM IS NOT SALVATION Did the river water make Jesus the Son of God? No. Did John the baptizer make Him Jesus? No. Neither does baptism make us Christians. No act of man is involved in salvation. Read these verses: "that if you confess with your mouth the Lord Jesus Christ and believe in your heart that God raised Him from the dead, you will be saved. For with the heart one believes unto righteousness, and with the mouth confession is made unto salvation. For 'whoever calls on the name of the LORD shall be saved'" (Romans 10:9-10, 13).

BAPTISM IS COMMANDED In Matthew 28:18-20, Jesus commands baptism in the Great Commission. Part of the Christian's role in leading people to Christ is pointing them to baptism after salvation. Baptism naturally follows salvation, but it is secondary in importance.

> "Baptism, whether a spoonful or a tankful,
> can never save anybody. You are saved
> by trusting Jesus." ADRIAN ROGERS

RESOURCE: Listen to Adrian Rogers' message, *Start Right: Believer's Baptism.*

HOW DO I KNOW GOD REALLY LOVES ME?

"We love Him because He first loved us" (1 John 4:19).

"For God so loved the world that He gave His only begotten Son, that whoever believes in Him should not perish but have everlasting life" (John 3:16).

It was God who loved you first. One of the wonders of salvation is that our sin did not deter His love for us, but instead caused Him to prove His love for us. Romans 5:8 says, "But God demonstrates His own love toward us, in that while we were still sinners, Christ died for us." Jesus said in John 10:11, "I am the good shepherd. The good shepherd gives His life for the sheep." No one made Jesus give His life and no one took His life from Him. He willingly gave it for you. John 10:17-18a reminds us, "Therefore My Father loves Me, because I lay down My life that I may take it again. No one takes it from Me, but I lay it down of Myself." This loving and willing sacrifice paid the penalty that sin brought.

We all have sinned—every one of us. Romans 3:23 says, "For all have sinned and fall short of the glory of God." Because of our sin, what we have earned, and what we deserve, is death—physical and spiritual eternal death. However, God offers the gift of eternal life through the sacrifice Jesus made. Romans 6:23 gives us the good news: "For the wages of sin is death, but the gift of God is eternal life through Jesus Christ our Lord." Then, to further prove His love and His desire to have a personal relationship with each of us, He didn't sit back to see what we would we do. He pursued us! In John 6:44a, Jesus said, "No one can come to Me unless the Father who sent Me draws him." What an amazing God and Savior! To know that we would not pursue Him in our sinfulness, and yet choose to pursue us anyway! Wow! God loves you, God sacrificed Himself for you, and God has pursued you!

> "A man will go to Hell unsaved, but he will never go unloved." ADRIAN ROGERS

RESOURCE: Listen to the message, *When You Doubt God's Love.*

HOW DO I START A RELATIONSHIP WITH GOD?

"For 'whoever Whoever calls on the name of the Lord shall be saved'" (Romans 10:13).

Even as complicated as Scripture can seem, salvation is one of those areas that is clear as glass. God wanted to make sure of that because God desires a personal relationship with you. Once you recognize yourself as a sinner in need of a Savior, you simply accept the free gift of salvation God offers, which Jesus paid for on the cross. Ephesians 2:8-9 says, "For by grace you have been saved through faith, and that not of yourselves; it is the gift of God, not of works, lest anyone should boast." When we admit to God that we are sinners, understand we cannot save ourselves, and acknowledge that Jesus died to pay the penalty for our sins and was raised from the dead on the third day, we receive His salvation. We are reconciled with God. "For I delivered to you first of all that which I also received; that Christ died for our sins according to the Scriptures, and that He was buried, and that He rose again the third day according to the Scriptures" (1 Corinthians 15:3-4). "...that if you confess with your mouth the Lord Jesus and believe in your heart that God has raised Him from the dead, you will be saved" (Romans 10:9).

To begin the sweetest relationship you will ever know, all you must do for Him to save you is ask. Simply pray something similar to this:

"Dear God, I know that You love me, and I know that You want to save me. Jesus, You died to save me. You promised to save me if I would trust You. I do trust You. By faith I receive You as my Lord and Savior. Forgive my sin. Cleanse me. Save me, Lord Jesus. Thank You for salvation. I receive it by faith like a child, and that settles it. Now begin to make me the person you want me to be, and help me, Lord Jesus, never to be ashamed of You. Amen."

"Oh the love that thought it; oh the grace that brought it!" ADRIAN ROGERS

RESOURCE: Listen to Pastor Rogers' message, *The Simplicity of Salvation*.

HOW CAN I BE SURE I'M SAVED?

"Who is he who overcomes the world, but he who believes that Jesus is the Son of God?" (1 John 5:5).

One of God's promises is the assurance of our salvation. First John 5 reveals the basis for our belief, and how to be absolutely sure of our salvation in Jesus Christ.

THE ATONING WORK OF CHRIST First John 5:6a says, "This is he who came by water and blood—Jesus Christ..." Jesus took our sin to the cross, and with His blood, He paid sin's penalty. The water speaks of that which continues to cleanse. This assures us, not only of our salvation but also of our sanctification—His continuing work in our lives. He saves us from wrath and makes us pure.

THE ABIDING WITNESS OF THE SPIRIT The Holy Spirit takes the atoning work and He testifies of it. He gives witness to us and in us. "It is the Spirit who bears witness, because the Spirit is truth" (1 John 5:6b). Before we're even saved, the Holy Spirit is telling us about Jesus. And when we receive Christ, He comes into us, and witnesses from within. "He who believes in the Son of God has the witness in himself" (1 John 5:10a). The Spirit also witnesses through us. When we are sure of our salvation, we can witness to others, because we know that our witness is not dependent on eloquence or logic, but upon the Spirit.

THE ASSURANCE OF THE WORD OF THE FATHER God gave us His Word. If you take a red pen to 1 John and circle the word "know," you'll find it more than forty times. That's certainty. It's not a hope-so salvation but a *know-so* salvation, so you can say, "No matter what happens, I am reconciled with God. I know I'm Heaven-born and Heaven-bound."

"We do not live by explanations; we live by promises." ADRIAN ROGERS

RESOURCE: Watch the message, *How to be Absolutely Sure.*

CAN CHRISTIANS LOSE THEIR SALVATION?

**"For the death He died, He died to sin once for all"
(Romans 6:10a).**

Can Christians lose their salvation? Absolutely not! There are two things Christians can know for sure about salvation. We can know that we are His, and we can know that we cannot lose our salvation because we are reconciled with God. These assurances are found directly in Scripture.

WE ARE HIS "And this is the testimony, that God has given us eternal life, and this life is in His Son. He who has the Son has life; he who does not have the Son of God does not have life. These things have I written to you who believe in the name of the Son of God, that you may know that you have eternal life, and that you may continue to believe in the name of the Son of God" (1 John 5:11-13).

This passage tells us we have a know-so salvation. If we have repented of our sin and accepted Jesus as Savior, God has given us eternal life.

SALVATION IS FOREVER "And I give them eternal life, and they shall never perish; neither shall anyone snatch them out of My hand. My Father, who has given them to me, is greater than all; and no one is able to snatch them out of My Father's hand. I and My Father are one" (John 10:28-30).

This passage tells us that once we are His, no one is able to take us from Him. No other person or spiritual foe can take us away from the Lord God. Furthermore, we cannot take ourselves away from God. Our salvation is not based on what we do or don't do. It's solely based on God Himself. Therefore, we can do nothing to receive it, nor can we do anything to lose it.

"Do you think God brought you that far, that God has so much invested in you, that after having died for you, He's going to abandon you?" ADRIAN ROGERS

RECOMMENDED: Get the book, "Discover Jesus: The Author and Finisher of Our Faith."

NOW THAT I'M SAVED, WHAT'S NEXT?

"Therefore, if anyone is in Christ, he is a new creation; old things have passed away; behold, all things have become new" (2 Corinthians 5:17).

If you recently trusted Jesus Christ as your personal Savior you are now reconciled with God. You might be wondering, "Now what do I do?"

Salvation is the beginning, not the end. Your sins have been forgiven, your name is written in God's book in Heaven (your eternal destiny), and you have the Holy Spirit within you—your body is His temple. Now the Christian life begins. Second Peter 3:18 says that you are to "...grow in the grace and knowledge of our Lord and Savior Jesus Christ" (2 Peter 3:18a).

FIRST STEP Find a Gospel-centered, Bible-preaching church. You are to be worshipping and fellowshipping with other believers.

SECOND STEP Next is believer's baptism, which is an act of obedience. Baptism does not save you; it does not wash away sins. You've already been saved and your sins have been removed. Psalm 103:12 says, "As far as the east is from the west, so far has He removed our transgressions from us." Rather, baptism is symbolic of Jesus' death, burial and resurrection. Your baptism shows others that you have died to your old life and have been raised to live a new life in Christ.

THIRD STEP God would have you begin reading and studying His Word, the Bible. When it comes to reading the

Bible, it's better to start small and be consistent than to try to read too much and burn out. Find an amount you can read consistently and try to stick with it as much as possible. The more consistent you are with reading the Bible, the more you'll grow as a Christian.

If you're new to studying the Bible, you may want to start with the Book of John which tells of what Jesus did and said. From there, consider reading sections in both the Old and New Testaments. This will help you understand the big picture of how God is at work in the world. While you read the Bible, ask God to teach you His ways and give you understanding. Ask Him to help you observe His words with your whole heart. You can be absolutely sure He will answer this prayer.

> "I read other books. The Bible
> reads me." ADRIAN ROGERS

RECOMMENDED: Love Worth Finding would like to provide you with free resources to help you grow in your faith. Fill out the short form and we'll respond.

RESOURCE: Access "The Ultimate Guide to Bible Study."

Pastor **Adrian Rogers'** unique ability to apply biblical truth to everyday life is yet unparalleled by other modern teachers. **Love Worth Finding** is dedicated to glorifying God by honoring that legacy and expanding his impact.

LWF produces broadcast, print and digital media that reaches around the globe with the profound truth of the Gospel, simply stated. **The mission: to bring people to Christ and mature them in the faith.**

WILL YOU SUPPORT LOVE WORTH FINDING?

LWF is funded primarily through gifts from Christians committed to sharing God's Word with lost and hurting people from all walks of life.

lwf.org/give

or call 800-274-5673